AF270407

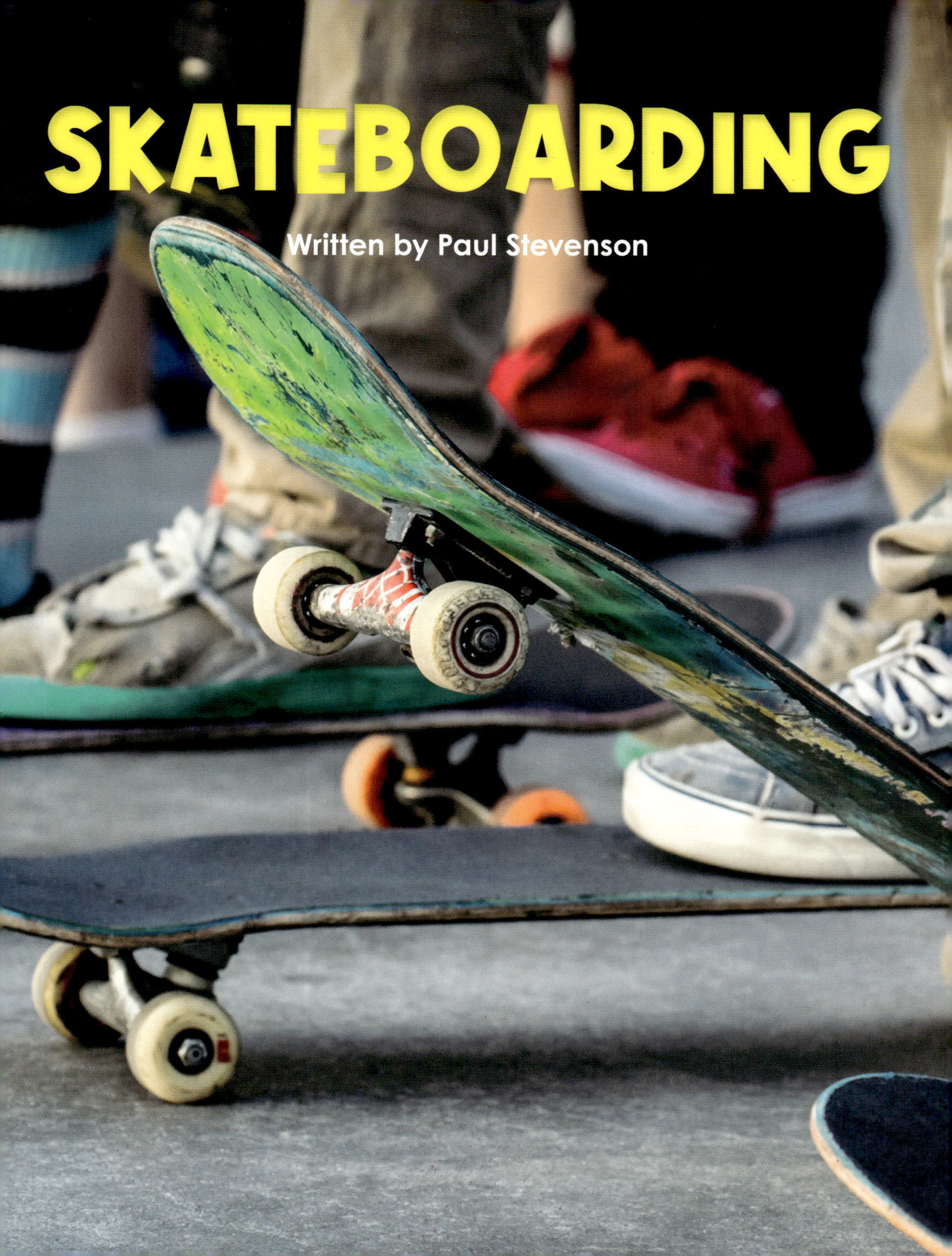

SKATEBOARDING
Written by Paul Stevenson

# CONTENTS




First published in 2024 by
Hungry Tomato Ltd
F15, Old Bakery Studios,
Blewetts Wharf, Malpas Road,
Truro, Cornwall,
TR1 1QH, UK.





A CIP catalog record for this book is available from the
British Library.

ISBN 9781915461919
Manufactured in the USA

Discover more at
www.hungrytomato.com

## DISCLAIMER:

The tricks featured in this book have
been performed by experienced
skateboarders. Neither the publisher nor
the author shall be liable for any bodily
harm or damage to property that may
happen as a result of trying the tricks in
this book.

In many places, it is illegal to skateboard.
Look out for signs. Don't break the law.

All words in **BOLD** can be found in the glossary.

# THE HIDDEN WORLD OF SKATEBOARDING

Skateboarding has its own language. It has its own heroes. It also has its own music, video games and its own art - **graffiti**.

Skateboarding will change the way that you look at the streets. Welcome to the fantastic world of skateboarding!

# THEN...

## Skateboarding was invented in the late 1950s-1960s in the USA.

Bored surfers began skateboarding when there were no waves out at sea. They **carved** up the streets of California. Soon an army of skateboarders grew!

In 1963, the first skateboarding contest was held. Skaters started to invent tricks and flips.

Skateboarding appeared in magazines and TV shows, which made it even more popular

Skateboarding was even in the 1970s TV show *Wonder Woman*

The **ollie** is the most important trick to learn. It was invented by Alan "Ollie" Gelfand in the late 1970s. You need to ollie to be able to do most tricks.



## HOW TO DO AN OLLIE?

Kick down on the tail of the board. At the same time, drag your front foot up the middle of the board. As you do this, you must jump as well.

# NOW...

**Now people skateboard all over the world!**

Many skateboarders are **professional**. This means they earn money doing it!

Skateboarding has even become an Olympic sport. The world's best skaters competed for the first time in the 2020 games.

All skaters want to break a world record!

YO 2020

**DID YOU KNOW?**

- Fastest speed: 89mph
- Highest air: 25 feet (7.6m)

# DECKS

The graphics on skateboard decks are changing all the time. Professional riders choose their own unique design.

The **graphics** on your deck can tell other riders something about your style and who you are.

# STREET STYLE

Many people start **ripping up** the streets when they first discover skateboarding. They use street furniture to do tricks.

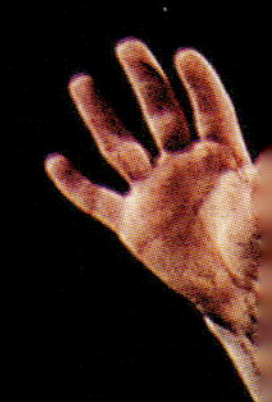

## SKATESPEAK

Street furniture is skatespeak for curbs, park benches, stairs and handrails.

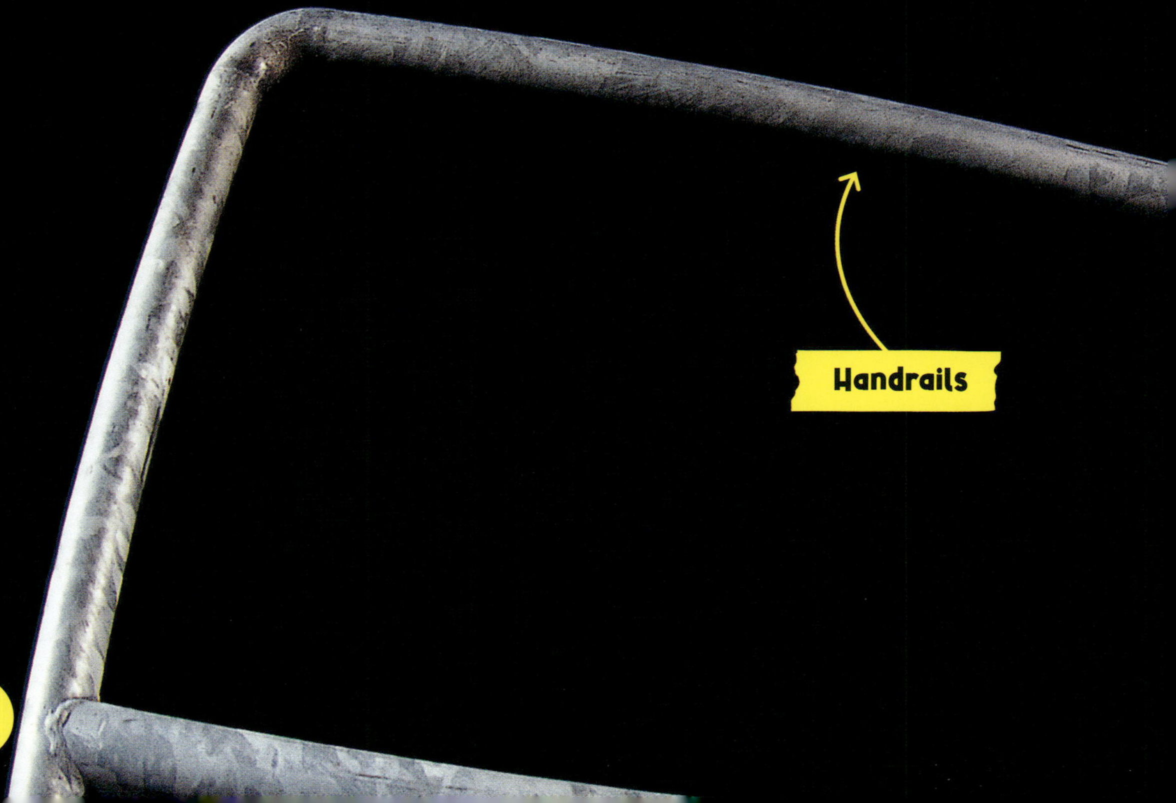

Street decks are thin and small with small, light wheels.

# PARK LIFE

**Many towns have skateparks with halfpipes, bowls and other obstacles.**

Skateboarders use the **obstacles** to perform flips, spins and grabs high in the air.

**Skateparks** are ideal places to **hook up** with friends. You can show off your new tricks. You can also see local heroes **killing it** on the obstacles.

# HALFPIPES

Halfpipes allow the skater to move back and forth between the two arched ramps. They use halfpipes to pick up speed and do tricks and flips.

# BOWLS

Bowls look a bit like empty swimming pools. Skaters use bowls to catch speed without coming down onto flat ground.

# SPINE RAMPS

Spine ramps are great for freestyle skaters looking to do jumps, tricks and flips, mid-air.

# RAMP IT UP

A vert ramp is a big halfpipe about 11 feet (3.5m) high. Helmets and pads are a must for all types of skateboarding.

Vert ramps are where skateboarders learn to fly!

Rexona
Elbow pads
Helmet
Shorts allow the skater to wear knee pads
Vert decks are wider than street decks. This gives better control and stability
Big wheels gain more speed. They also help when touching back down to earth!

# FROM THE GROUND UP

**Once you are comfortable riding around, the ollie is the first trick you need to learn.**

It's the base you need to build on for further skateboard tricks, such as flips and grinds. When you can do these, you will be a great skateboarder.

## KICKFLIP

A kickflip is where the board spins 360 degrees around its length underneath you. After it has spun, you need to land back on the board.

# GRIND

To perform a grind, you must rub your **trucks** across a rail. When both trucks are grinding, you are doing a 50–50 grind.

## SKATESPEAK

Fakie – Traveling backward.
Gnarly – Dangerous or extreme.
Goofy – Standing right foot forward.
Rad – Really good.
Regular – Standing left foot forward.
Ripping – Skateboarding very well.
Sick – Good.
Slam – When you fall off your board.

# FLIPS

They take lots of repetition to master but look very cool.

## 360°

The board spins 360 degrees and flips at the same time.

# BACKSIDE FLIP

The board flips and turns 180 degrees. You follow the board and ride away backward.

# FAKIE KICKFLIP

This is a kickflip going backward.

# GRIND ON!

The trucks of your deck can be used to grind along edges and rails.

## IT'S A TRICKY COMBO OF POWER AND BALANCE!

## NOSE GRIND

A nose grind is when you rub just the front truck on a rail.

## SKATESPEAK

Here are some weird grind names:

- Willy grind
- Hurricane grind
- Sausage grind

# FEEBLE GRIND

A feeble grind is a tough trick. You need to position the front truck over the rail, while grinding only on the back truck.

# FOR THE EXPERTS

You may see some of these tricks in the streets and skateparks where you live. **TIME TO EXPLORE!**

## WALLRIDE TO FAKIE

Ramps will allow you to fly like a bird!

# KICKFLIP

Stairs are no longer just to walk up and down...

...some can kickflip over them!

# BOARDSLIDE

Handrails become train tracks for boardslides. Sliding the middle of your board across the rail looks pretty awesome!

# COMPETITIONS

Skateboarding has become a highly competitive sport.

Besides the Olympics, the other major skateboarding contests are the X Games and the World Skateboarding Championships. These are for professionals to show off their skills and tricks.

Watch skateboard superstars perform amazing tricks and compete to be named the winner!

You can also watch top skateboard team **demos**.

Maybe you'll even see someone break a world record!

# THE DREAM

Professional skateboarders get paid to skate! Getting sponsored is the first step toward a career as a pro.

The **sponsorship** company will send the pro skaters all over the world to enter competitions. They also get a board with their own **unique** graphics.

You have to be the best of the best to get sponsored.

In reality, very few people make lots of money just from skateboarding. People that do can become very famous, like Tony Hawk.

Tony Hawk at the Hall of Game Awards because of his video games, *Pro Skater 1 and 2*.

# SKATEBOARD HEROES

## TONY HAWK

**Tony Hawk has set up a foundation to help pay for skateboard parks in low-income areas in the USA.**

The Tony Hawk Foundation, now known as "The Skatepark Project", has raised over $11 million for skateparks in the USA.

So far, more than 650 skatepark projects have received funding from his foundation.

## DANNY WAY

In 2004, Danny Way broke his own world record for the longest skateboard jump. It's now set at 79 feet (24m)!

In 2005, Danny jumped across the Great Wall of China on a skateboard!

# GLOSSARY

**carve** - to turn sharply on your board.

**demo (demonstration)** - a skateboard team showing off their moves.

**graffiti** - eye-catching drawings and words created with spray paint.

**graphics** - the pictures or designs on the underside of the deck.

**hook up** - skatespeak for meeting up and spending time with friends.

**killing it** - skatespeak for skating at a very high standard.

**obstacles** - halfpipes, ramps, stairs – any object that you can skateboard on.

**ollie** - a skateboard jump. The ollie is the best way to get all four wheels off the ground. Hit the tail and jump in the air.

**professional** - the best of the best! Skateboarders who received sponsorship (see right) by a skateboard company.

**ripping up** - skatespeak for skating really well.

**skateparks** - indoor or outdoor parks designed for skateboarding. Obstacles in the park can be made from concrete, wood and sometimes even metal.

**sponsorship** - when a company gives a skateboarder free stuff, such as decks. If you are really good, a company may pay you to skate for them and advertise their products.

**stability** - making something stable so it isn't wobbly.

**trucks** - the metal parts that fix the wheels to the deck.

**unique** - the only one of its kind.

# INDEX




Picture credits:

(t=top; b=bottom; c=center; l=left; r=right):
Shutterstock: 2-3, 8c, 11t. Hurricanehank 11br, 25; Israfoto 14b; Underworld 15t; Aldo_Parrotta 15bl; Victoria Prokhun 15br; Maciej Kopaniecki 21br; Joshua Sanderson Media 27t; Hafizzuddin 27br; Arturo verea 28-29; S_bukley 29tl, 30tr; Kathy Hutchins 30bl; FiledIMAGE 1, 31b; A.Einsiedler 16, 17; YanLev 8-9. Everett Collection/ Rex Features: 6b. Ben Molyneux/ Alamy: 10. Andrew Horsley: 4-5, 7, 12-13, 18-19, 20b, 21c, 22b, 23t, 23b, 24b, 26b.

Every effort has been made to trace the copyright holders, and we apologize in advance for any unintentional omissions. We would be pleased to insert the appropriate acknowledgments in any subsequent edition of this publication.